STEM Careers

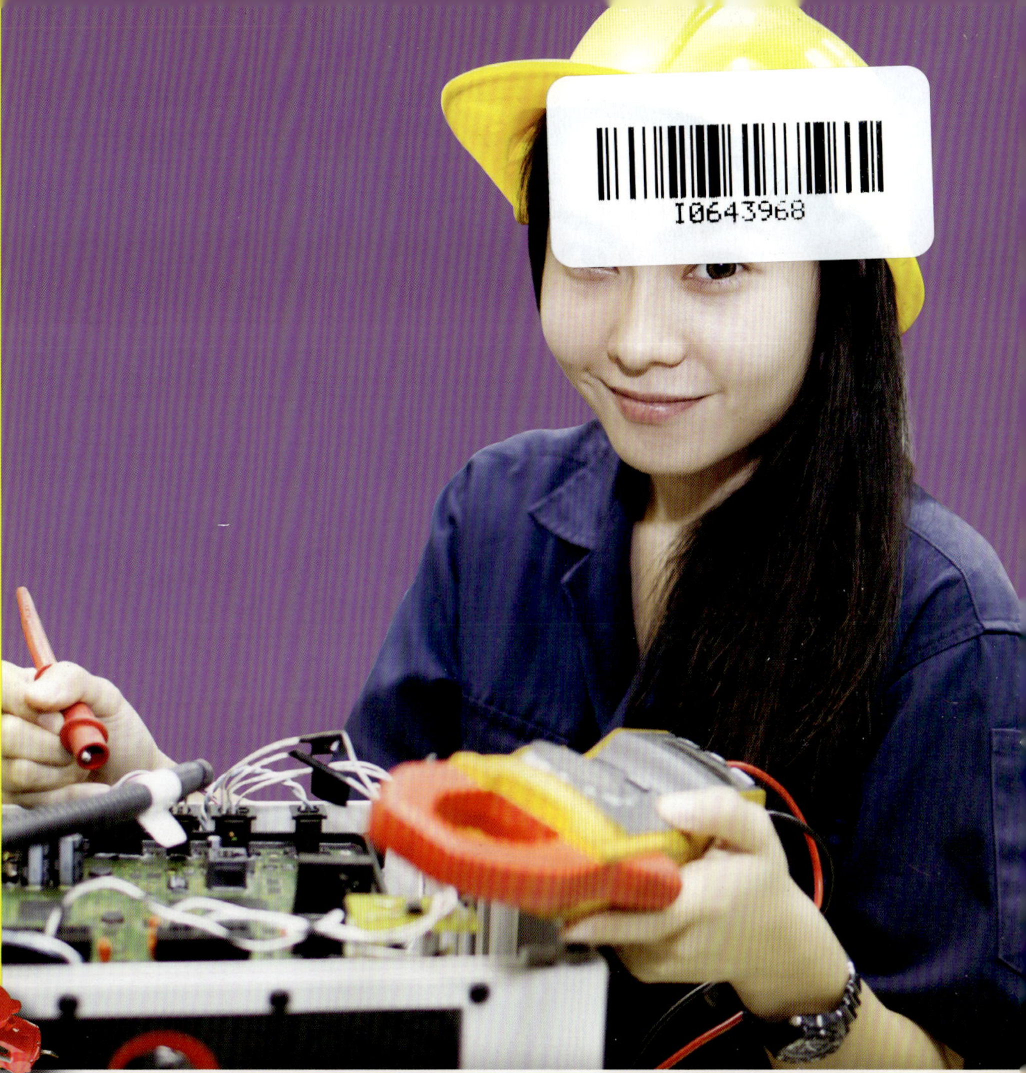

MECHANICAL ENGINEER

Joy Gregory

AV2
www.av2books.com

Step 1
Go to **www.av2books.com**

Step 2
Enter this unique code
QLFOTPW9L

Step 3
Explore your interactive eBook!

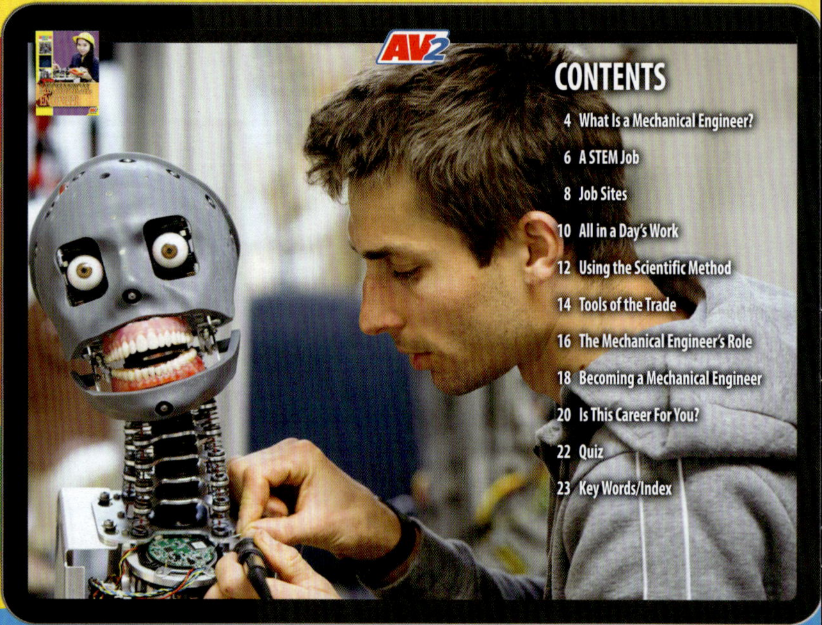

AV2 is optimized for use on any device

Your interactive eBook comes with...

Contents
Browse a live contents page to easily navigate through resources

Audio
Listen to sections of the book read aloud

Videos
Watch informative video clips

Weblinks
Gain additional information for research

Try This!
Complete activities and hands-on experiments

Key Words
Study vocabulary, and complete a matching word activity

Quizzes
Test your knowledge

Slideshows
View images and captions

... and much, much more!

View new titles and product videos at www.av2books.com

STEM Careers

MECHANICAL ENGINEER

Contents

AV2 Book Code 2
What Is a Mechanical Engineer? 4
A STEM Job 6
Job Sites 8
All in a Day's Work 10
Using the Scientific Method 12
Tools of the Trade 14
The Mechanical Engineer's Role 16
Becoming a Mechanical Engineer 18
Is This Career For You? 20
Quiz 22
Key Words/Index 23

What Is a Mechanical Engineer?

Engineers are people who solve everyday problems. They create things that move people and products from one place to another. Their inventions make life better for people.

The first mechanical engineers invented spoons and hammers. They made machines that could lift and pull heavy objects. Early mechanical engineers would have also played a key role in developing the wheel and axle, which are now used on vehicles worldwide.

Today's mechanical engineers design and build complex tools and machines. Some of their machines power engines. Others harvest farmers' crops. Mechanical engineers work in the **aerospace** and **construction** industries. They design the machines used in factories. Some of them build computers and cars.

The **American Society of Mechanical Engineers** was founded in **1880**.

ASME
SETTING THE STANDARD

In **2020**, *U.S. News and World Report* **ranked** mechanical engineering **#1** on its **best engineering jobs** list.

#1

There are about **307,000 mechanical engineers** working in the **United States**.

Mechanical engineers working in the aerospace industry are often responsible for developing and testing materials.

A STEM Job

Mechanical engineers work in the field of STEM. STEM stands for Science, Technology, Engineering, and Mathematics, or math. Demand for workers with STEM training is high. Many workplaces hire people with a variety of STEM skills.

Mechanical engineers hold different STEM jobs. Many specialize in a particular kind of science. They might work in medical science, helping to develop equipment. Some work in aviation science, where they contribute to the design and construction of airplanes. All mechanical engineers use math to do their jobs.

Where Mechanical Engineers Work

Mechanical engineers work in every U.S. state. Michigan tops the list of states with the most mechanical engineers. California, Texas, Pennsylvania, and Ohio also employ large numbers of mechanical engineers.

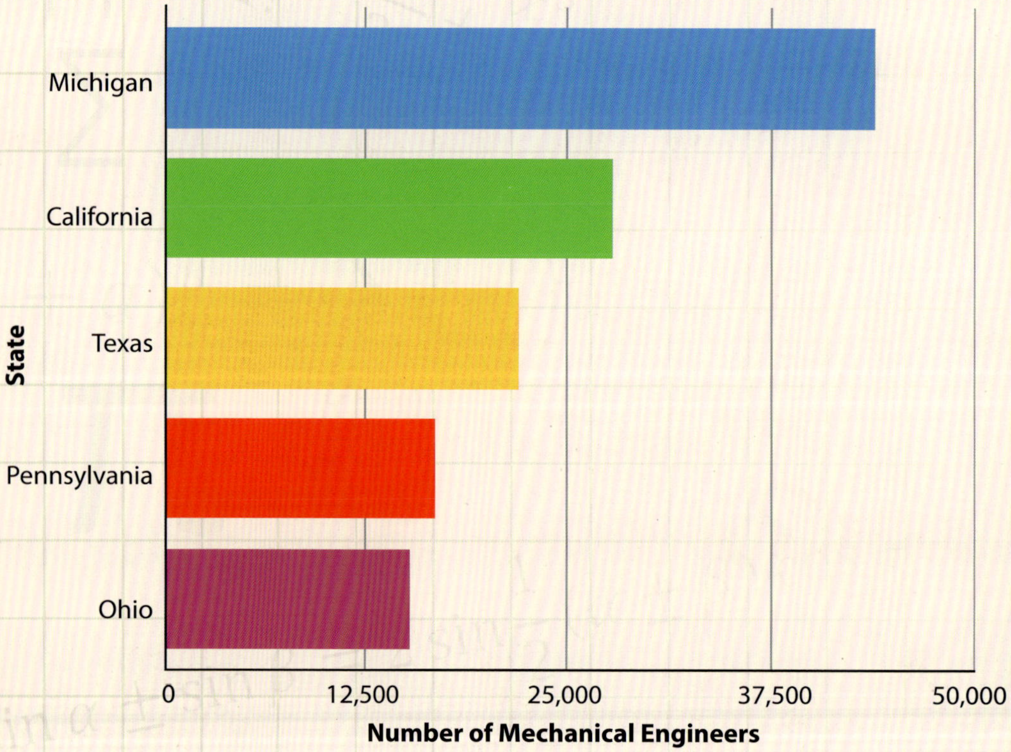

Many mechanical engineers use STEM skills to invent new technology. These can include everyday items, such as motorcycles and refrigerators. Others invent machines for scientific use. Some mechanical engineers work in factories. They use their STEM skills to run machines.

Mechanical engineers work to improve human productivity through the use of machines. They can be found developing automated technology that helps get work done efficiently.

STEM

Mechanical engineers make up about **20 %** of all engineers working in the **United States**.

As **a group**, engineers earn more **than 2x** the **national average** of other workers.

1 in **5** mechanical engineers works in **building construction** and **design**.

Job Sites

Most mechanical engineers work inside buildings. A mechanical engineer at a hospital may monitor and repair the **ventilation system**. At a clothing factory, mechanical engineers work with people who run machines that sew fabric. Some mechanical engineers work for companies that deliver electricity or natural gas to people's homes. Railroad companies hire mechanical engineers to make sure the trains work.

Engineering Work Sites in the United States

Mechanical engineers work for government agencies and private companies. They often work alongside people in scientific fields, performing **experiments** in research **laboratories**.

Microsoft
Redmond, Washington

NASA Jet Propulsion Laboratory
Pasadena, California

Some mechanical engineers do research for companies. They make machines faster and more energy efficient. Others make airplanes and cars safer. Governments also hire mechanical engineers to do research. Mechanical engineers build government satellites. Some mechanical engineers work for the military.

The U.S. automotive industry also employs mechanical engineers. Many of them work at automotive plants. They design the cars and trucks built in the United States. These engineers test vehicles for safety and performance.

Ford Global Technologies LLC
Dearborn, Michigan

Lockheed Martin Corporation
Bethesda, Maryland

Mechanical engineers invent devices that help people with spinal cord injuries regain the use of their limbs.

All in a Day's Work

A mechanical engineer's daily work depends on where he or she is employed. Mechanical engineers in the construction industry may spend part of their day reading **blueprints**. They advise builders on how and where to install machines such as furnaces. Other mechanical engineers help **architects** design buildings. These engineers know how much space each staircase needs. They may also give advice about building materials.

Mechanical engineers in research jobs spend their days experimenting and developing technology that helps others. Some invent technology that will help people with disabilities. This can include **prosthetic** limbs and wheelchairs. It can also involve creating street-crossing signs that flash lights and make noise. Other researchers invent items that make **renewable energy**. They may develop and test solar panels and wind turbines.

Sample Daily Schedule

Mechanical engineers spend most of their day working with tools and machines. Some specialize in machine repair. Others train the people who operate the equipment that builds new machines.

8:00 AM

A mechanical engineer arrives at his office in an automobile manufacturing plant. He reviews the drawings for a new truck design and makes notes about a design problem that should be fixed.

9:00 AM

The mechanical engineer meets with the design team. He shows them a study. It says back-up cameras are better when mounted high. The designers agree to move the camera in a new car they are developing.

11:00 AM

The engineer is called to a research lab where windshield glass is being tested. The test machine has stopped working. He puts on his safety glasses and hard hat. The people who operate the test machine show him the problem. The engineer calls for a repair crew.

1:00 PM

The repair crew arrives at the lab. The mechanical engineer shows the crew the broken part. They take out their tools and begin to fix the machine.

3:00 PM

The repair crew tests the machine. It is now working the way it should. The mechanical engineer calls the machine operators. He explains what the crew did to fix the machine.

4:00 PM

The mechanical engineer returns to his office. He writes a report about the problem in the research lab. The report lists three new steps machine operators must follow. These steps will prevent future breakdowns.

Using the Scientific Method

Scientists use the scientific method to solve problems. The scientific method is a series of steps. It begins with a question scientists want to answer. First, the scientists find out if someone else has asked the same question. If so, they review that scientist's results and gather information for their work. Next, they make a hypothesis. This is what they think the answer to their question will be. The scientists then test the hypothesis with an experiment. After the experiment, they form a conclusion. This means they study the results and decide if the question was answered. Finally, the scientists share the results with the public and other scientists.

1. Ask a Question

Does the amount of air in a basketball affect its bounce?

2. Construct a Hypothesis

Some basketballs bounce higher than others. Bounce is affected by the amount of air inside the ball. This supports the hypothesis that basketballs bounce higher when full of air.

3. Test with an Experiment

Use an air pump to fill one basketball. Let some air out of a second ball. Drop each ball to the floor from the same height. Record how high each basketball bounces. Repeat three times.

4. Did the Test Work?

The basketball with less air did not bounce as high as the one full of air. This demonstrates how air pressure inside a ball affects its bounce.

5. Draw Conclusions

When air is pumped inside a ball, the air squeezes together. This creates pressure inside the ball. Balls with more pressure bounce higher.

Tools of the Trade

Mechanical engineers need precision tools. Precision tools measure with great accuracy. Many have steel parts. This makes them last a long time.

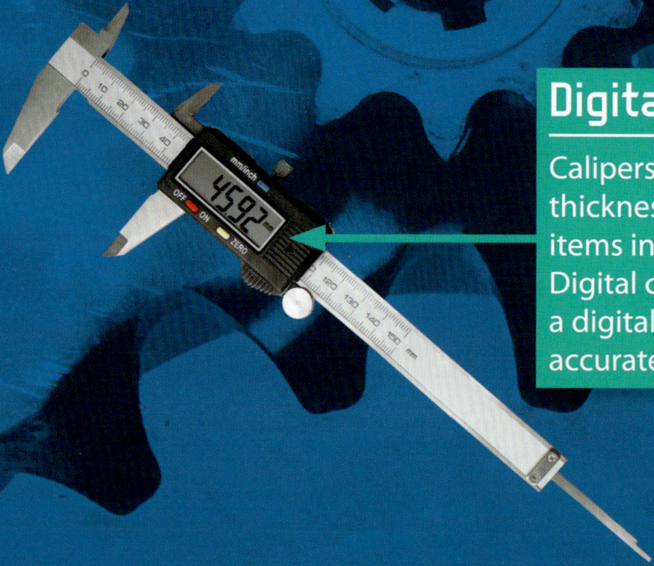

Digital Calipers

Calipers are a measuring tool. They measure thickness and **diameter**. Calipers can measure items in fractions of inches (centimeters). Digital calipers show measurements on a digital screen. They are faster and more accurate than traditional calipers.

Gauge Blocks

Gauge blocks are used to make sure that a mechanical engineer's measuring tools are accurate. Made of steel or ceramic, they are manufactured to exact sizes. Gauge blocks can be squares or rectangles. Some are angles. The sizes and angles are based on international standards. Gauge blocks can also be used to measure parts accurately.

Flow Meters

Mechanical engineers use flow meters to test pipes. These tools measure the volume or mass of a liquid or gas flowing through the pipe. Natural gas will move through a pipe at a different rate than water. Water flows at a different rate than oil. Flow meters help mechanical engineers design the right pipe for the right product.

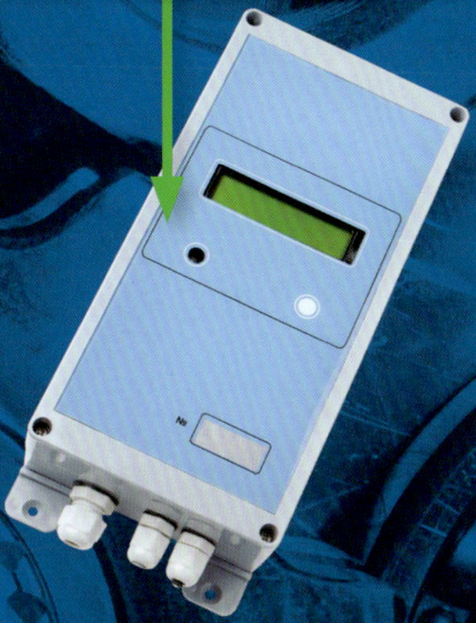

Force Gauge

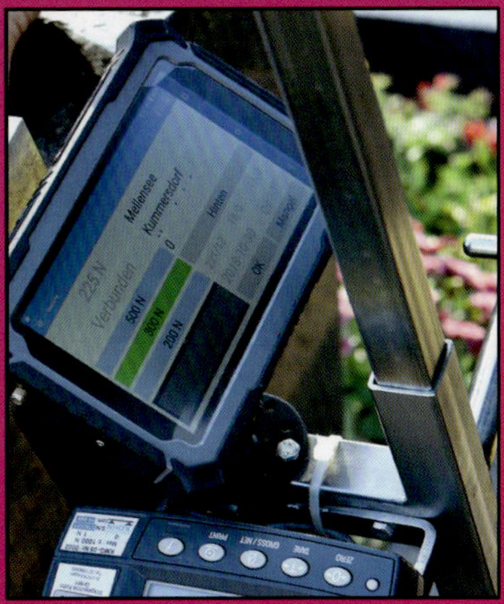

A force gauge measures how much force it takes to break something. In the research lab, it is used in push and pull tests. It tests parts such as wires or pipes. Mechanical engineers use the force gauge to test how long a part will last and if it will work for its intended use.

Steel Story

Steel adds strength to many of the things mechanical engineers build. Made mainly of **iron ore** and **carbon**, steel holds up buildings and bridges. Steel parts also hold machines together.

Then

Steel was invented in the 13th century BC. Until the 1700s AD, steel was mostly used to make weapons. In 1712, Thomas Newcomen built the first steam engine using steel parts. Cheaper steel production and the steam engine led to the **Industrial Revolution**.

Now

Today, steel is used to make a variety of items. Wind turbines and cell phone towers both contain steel. The containers that transport grain, oil, and food are made of steel. Steel is also used to make nuts, bolts, and screws.

The Mechanical Engineer's Role

Mechanical engineers are trained to help people live, work, and play. Every industry benefits from their skills. The first mechanical engineers invented tools that made people more powerful. They proved that a rock tied to a stick made a better hammer than a plain rock. They invented new tools, such as the wheel. Over time, these engineers combined their tools to invent new machines. One of the first machines they invented was the pulley.

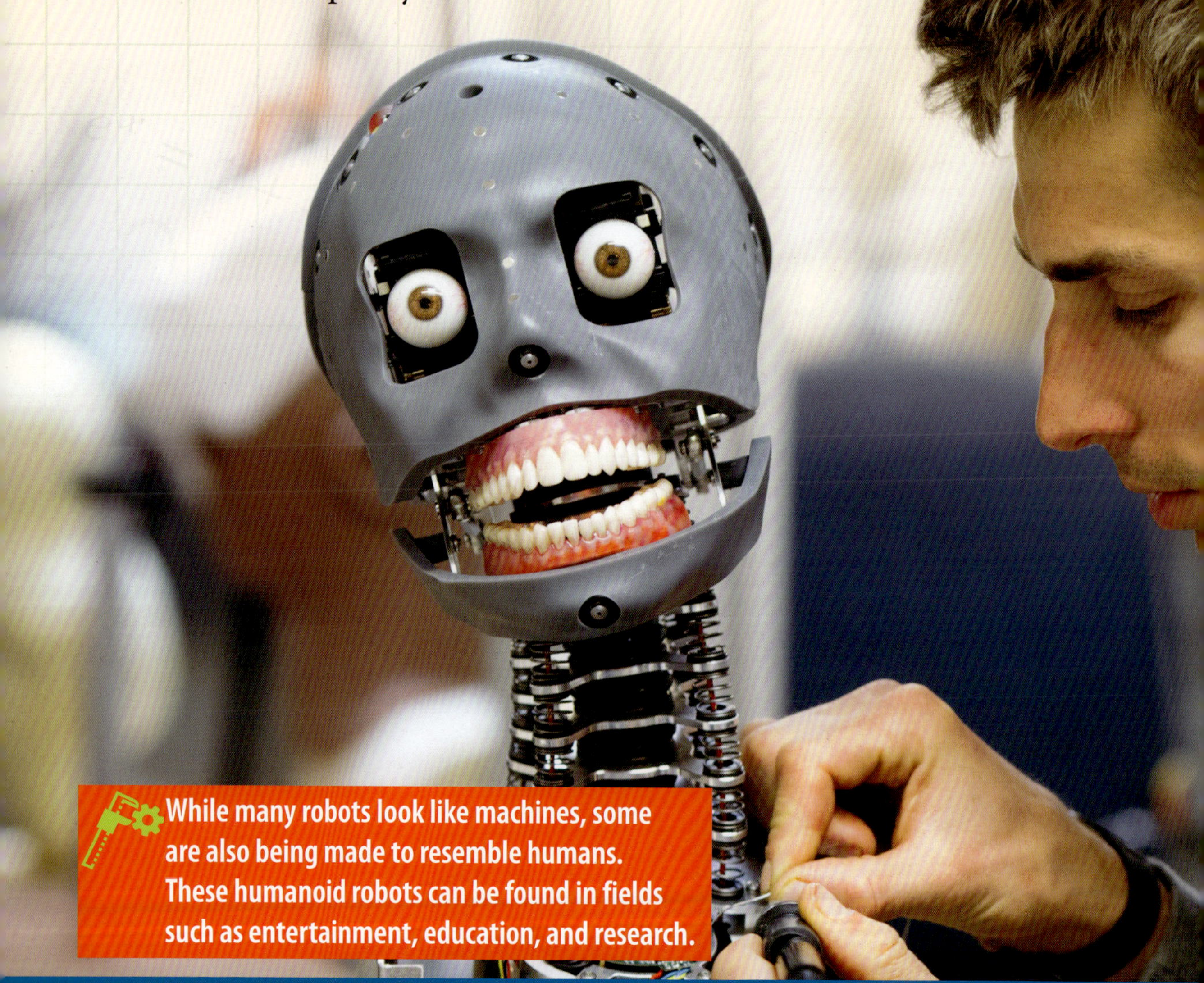

While many robots look like machines, some are also being made to resemble humans. These humanoid robots can be found in fields such as entertainment, education, and research.

Today's mechanical engineers continue to invent things that help people. They build robots that can help people get work done more quickly and efficiently. They work with scientists to solve global problems, including **climate change**. These engineers design equipment, such as wind turbines, that cuts **greenhouse gases**. Mechanical engineers also teach people how machines work. Some of these machines are used to grow food or save water.

Robotics

Robots have become valuable to workplaces ranging from homes to manufacturing plants. Some are used to vacuum carpets. Others work in factories. Here, robots may do jobs such as drilling holes or tightening screws.

There are currently more than **1.6 million** robots **working** for industries **worldwide**.

The **1st** robot vacuum appeared in **1996**. Millions are now in use.

Robots at some warehouses can package up to **700 boxes per hour**.

Becoming a Mechanical Engineer

Future mechanical engineers like to work with machines. They enjoy fixing their own bicycles and taking apart old computers. At school, they do science projects that show how machines work. Would-be mechanical engineers read about inventors and inventions. They visit museums and science centers to see old and new machines. These students watch videos that show people how to repair appliances.

In high school, future mechanical engineers study math. They take classes in advanced math, such as algebra, as well as **physics** and computer science. These students often enroll in applied technology classes. Here, students have the opportunity to practice what they learn. Classes may focus on small engine repair, electronics, or automobiles.

Mechanical Engineer Salaries

Mechanical engineers make an average of $93,540 a year. Some industries pay more than others.

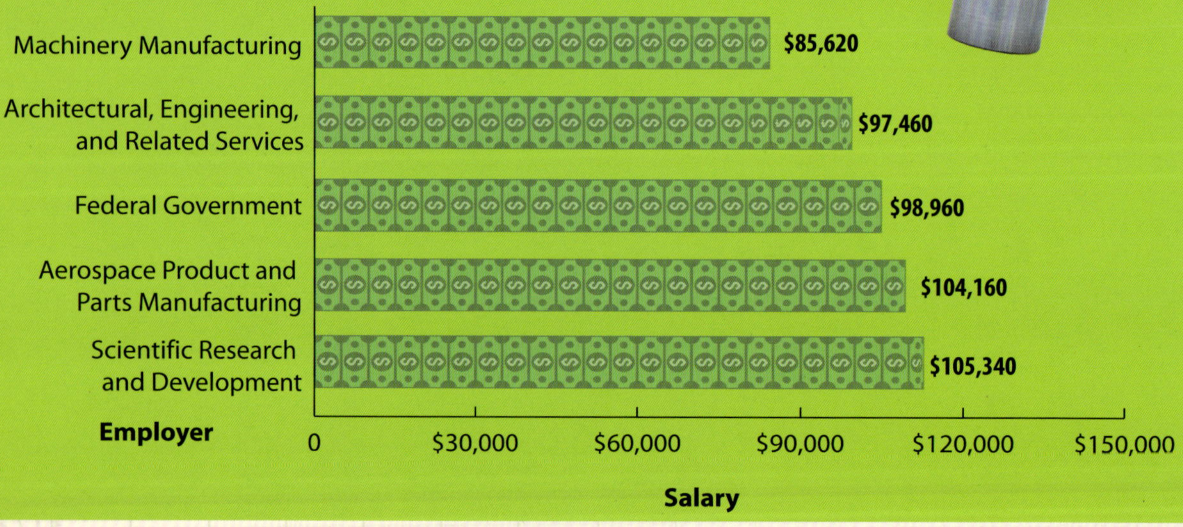

Mechanical engineers are known for their curiosity and interest in how things work.

Is This Career For You?

Mechanical engineers like to work with their hands. They enjoy math. At college, mechanical engineering students study math and science. They take lab classes, where they often participate in team projects. Students practice what they learn in class. They learn how to test ideas with experiments.

✓ Training

A mechanical engineer's formal training starts in college. Students learn to design and build machines. In labs, they learn to use precision tools. Many mechanical engineering students do **internships**. During an internship, the student works for an engineering company.

✓ Education

Mechanical engineers have a **bachelor's degree**. This takes at least four years to complete. Students may then study for an advanced degree. That can take another two to seven years to complete. Mechanical engineers with advanced degrees develop skills that can be used in specific fields, such as architecture or digital technology.

✓ Application

Check job websites for mechanical engineering posts. Look at jobs in the places where you want to live. Apply to jobs that match your education and work experience. Ask professors to be references. Employers call references to ask about your work habits.

Career Connections

Plan your mechanical engineering career with this activity. Follow the instructions in the steps below to complete the process of becoming a mechanical engineer.

A Find family friends or neighbors who work as mechanical engineers. Ask to meet with them. Learn what they like about their jobs.

B Attend college fairs at your high school. Learn which colleges teach mechanical engineering. Visit their displays. Ask them which high school classes you should take.

C Go to a job fair in the community. Find out which companies hire mechanical engineers. Talk to them about summer jobs and internships.

D Search the internet. Make a list of local companies that hire mechanical engineers. Send them an email. Ask for information about what mechanical engineers do at their companies.

1. Look for ways to build your mechanical engineering skills. Join a robotics club at your college. Attend lectures by scientists and inventors. Read about mechanical engineers.

2. Get some work experience. Volunteer to help a professor do research. Apply for research jobs at college. Sign up for internships with mechanical engineering firms.

3. Make a list of companies that hire mechanical engineers. Collect their contact information. Send them résumés of your education and work experience. Include references they can contact.

4. Learn how to prepare for a job interview. Research every company you apply to work at. Practice answering questions about why you want to work for that company.

Quiz

1. In what year was the American Society of Mechanical Engineers founded?

2. What does STEM stand for?

3. Where is the NASA Jet Propulsion Laboratory?

4. What is the last step in the scientific method?

5. When did Thomas Newcomen build the first steam engine?

6. What do calipers measure?

7. When did the first robotic vacuum make its appearance?

8. What are the main materials found in steel?

9. What is the device that measures the volume and mass of gases and liquids flowing through a pipe called?

10. About how many mechanical engineers work in the United States?

Answers

1. 1880
2. Science, Technology, Engineering and Mathematics
3. Pasadena, California
4. Form a conclusion
5. 1712
6. Thickness and diameter
7. 1996
8. Iron ore and carbon
9. Flow meter
10. About 307,000

Key Words

aerospace: the branch of technology related to space flight

architects: people who design buildings

bachelor's degree: the first level of a college program of study

blueprints: the detailed diagrams of something to be built

carbon: a chemical element that can be added to iron through heat to make steel

climate change: a long-term change in the average weather patterns

construction: the industry that builds structures, including buildings and roads

diameter: distance across a round object or space

experiments: tests used to discover or prove something

greenhouse gases: gases in Earth's atmosphere that trap heat

Industrial Revolution: a period of time in the late 18th century when the invention of powered machines changed how goods and services were made and delivered

internships: positions students take to gain experience, often unpaid

iron ore: a rock that holds iron

laboratories: rooms designed for scientific experiments

physics: the study of what things are made of and how they move

prosthetic: a replacement limb, such as an arm or leg

renewable energy: energy that comes from a source that is not depleted when used

ventilation system: technology that helps warm and cool air move through a building

Index

aerospace industry 4, 5, 6, 18
automotive industry 9

calipers 14, 22
construction industry 4, 7, 10

education 16, 18, 20, 21

flow meters 15, 22
force gauge 15
Ford Global Technologies LLC 9

gauge blocks 14

Lockheed Martin Corporation 9

Microsoft 8

NASA Jet Propulsion Laboratory 8, 22
Newcomen, Thomas 15, 22

research 8, 9, 10, 11, 15, 16, 18, 21
robots 16, 17, 21, 22

scientific method 12, 13, 22
steel 14, 15, 22
STEM 6, 7, 22

Published by AV2
14 Penn Plaza 9th Floor
New York, NY 10122
Website: www.av2books.com

Library of Congress Cataloging-in-Publication Data

Names: Gregory, Joy, author.
Title: Mechanical engineer / Joy Gregory.
Description: New York, NY : AV2, [2021] | Series: STEM careers | Includes index. | Audience: Ages 9-12. | Audience: Grades 4-6. |
Identifiers: LCCN 2019045361 (print) | LCCN 2019045362 (ebook) | ISBN 9781791116880 (library binding) | ISBN 9781791116897 (paperback) | ISBN 9781791116903 | ISBN 9781791116910
Subjects: LCSH: Mechanical engineering--Juvenile literature.
Classification: LCC TJ147 .G748 2021 (print) | LCC TJ147 (ebook) | DDC 621.023--dc23
LC record available at https://lccn.loc.gov/2019045361
LC ebook record available at https://lccn.loc.gov/2019045362

Printed in Guangzhou, China
1 2 3 4 5 6 7 8 9 0 24 23 22 21 20

052020
101119

Project Coordinator: Heather Kissock
Designer: Ana María Vidal

Every reasonable effort has been made to trace ownership and to obtain permission to reprint copyright material. The publishers would be pleased to have any errors or omissions brought to their attention so that they may be corrected in subsequent printings.

The publisher acknowledges Getty Images, iStock, and Shutterstock as its primary image suppliers for this title.